EMMANUEL JOSEPH

Confluence of Prosperity, Weaving Threads of Growth, Health, and Relationship Strengthening

Copyright © 2025 by Emmanuel Joseph

All rights reserved. No part of this publication may be reproduced, stored or transmitted in any form or by any means, electronic, mechanical, photocopying, recording, scanning, or otherwise without written permission from the publisher. It is illegal to copy this book, post it to a website, or distribute it by any other means without permission.

First edition

This book was professionally typeset on Reedsy. Find out more at reedsy.com

Contents

1. Chapter 1: The Foundations of Prosperity — 1
2. Chapter 2: The Role of Education in Growth — 3
3. Chapter 3: The Interconnection of Physical and Mental Health — 5
4. Chapter 4: Building Resilient Relationships — 7
5. Chapter 5: Economic Growth and Personal Prosperity — 9
6. Chapter 6: Health as a Cornerstone of Prosperity — 11
7. Chapter 7: The Power of Purpose — 13
8. Chapter 8: The Role of Community — 14
9. Chapter 9: The Balance of Work and Life — 16
10. Chapter 10: The Influence of Technology on Prosperity — 18
11. Chapter 11: The Impact of Environment on Well-being — 20
12. Chapter 12: Cultivating Mindfulness and Presence — 22
13. Chapter 13: The Journey of Personal Growth — 24
14. Chapter 14: The Importance of Gratitude — 26
15. Chapter 15: The Synergy of Growth, Health, and Relationships — 28

1

Chapter 1: The Foundations of Prosperity

In the quiet dawn of our existence, prosperity was more than material wealth. It was a state of being where mind, body, and spirit were in harmonious alignment. The foundations of prosperity lie in our ability to grow not just economically, but personally and spiritually. When we lay the groundwork for a life that is rich in learning, curiosity, and wonder, we begin to build the true essence of prosperity. The growth of our character and knowledge becomes the bedrock upon which we build our lives, ensuring a lasting and fulfilling journey.

Moreover, health plays a pivotal role in this foundation. A body nurtured with proper nutrition, exercise, and care allows us to pursue our goals with vigor and resilience. Health is the silent enabler, often taken for granted until it is compromised. It's the engine that drives our daily actions and ambitions. When we prioritize our physical well-being, we lay a strong foundation for achieving holistic prosperity.

Equally important is the strength of our relationships. Humans are inherently social beings, and our connections with others profoundly affect our sense of well-being and fulfillment. Building and maintaining strong, supportive relationships creates a network of mutual aid and encouragement. These bonds offer comfort during challenging times and amplify our joys, forming an essential part of our prosperity.

In conclusion, the foundations of prosperity are multifaceted, encompassing growth, health, and relationships. By focusing on these pillars, we create a balanced and sustainable approach to living a prosperous life. It's not about chasing wealth or accolades but about nurturing the different aspects of our existence to achieve a harmonious and fulfilling life.

2

Chapter 2: The Role of Education in Growth

Education is often heralded as the key to unlocking a prosperous future. It is the medium through which we acquire knowledge, develop critical thinking skills, and gain the tools necessary to navigate the complexities of life. From early childhood education to lifelong learning, the pursuit of knowledge is a continuous journey that fuels personal and professional growth.

The impact of education extends beyond individual growth to societal progress. Educated individuals contribute to their communities by sharing their knowledge and skills, driving innovation, and fostering social cohesion. When societies invest in education, they create a foundation for economic development and social stability, paving the way for collective prosperity.

Moreover, education fosters a sense of curiosity and a love for learning. It encourages us to question, explore, and seek new understandings. This intellectual stimulation enriches our lives, making us more adaptable and open to change. In a rapidly evolving world, the ability to learn and adapt is crucial for maintaining a prosperous life.

In addition to formal education, experiential learning plays a vital role in our growth. Life experiences, whether through travel, work, or personal challenges, offer invaluable lessons that shape our perspectives and resilience.

By embracing both formal and experiential learning, we equip ourselves with a well-rounded foundation for navigating life's complexities and achieving holistic prosperity.

3

Chapter 3: The Interconnection of Physical and Mental Health

The symbiotic relationship between physical and mental health is a cornerstone of true prosperity. Our physical health directly influences our mental well-being, and vice versa. A healthy body supports a healthy mind, enabling us to engage fully with life's opportunities and challenges.

Regular physical activity, balanced nutrition, and adequate rest are fundamental to maintaining good health. Exercise not only strengthens the body but also releases endorphins, which elevate mood and reduce stress. A nutritious diet fuels the body and mind, providing the energy needed to function optimally. Proper sleep restores and rejuvenates, ensuring we wake up refreshed and ready to tackle the day.

Mental health, in turn, affects our physical well-being. Chronic stress, anxiety, and depression can manifest as physical ailments, weakening the immune system and increasing susceptibility to illness. Addressing mental health issues with the same urgency as physical health concerns is crucial for overall well-being. Practices such as mindfulness, meditation, and therapy can help manage mental health, fostering resilience and emotional stability.

The interconnection of physical and mental health underscores the importance of a holistic approach to well-being. By nurturing both aspects, we create a foundation for a prosperous life. This balanced approach allows us to pursue our goals with vigor, maintain fulfilling relationships, and enjoy a sense of harmony and fulfillment.

4

Chapter 4: Building Resilient Relationships

Strong, resilient relationships are vital to our sense of well-being and prosperity. They provide support, encouragement, and a sense of belonging, enriching our lives in countless ways. Building and maintaining these relationships requires effort, understanding, and effective communication.

The cornerstone of resilient relationships is trust. Trust is built through consistent, honest communication and mutual respect. It allows individuals to feel secure and valued, fostering a deep connection. When trust is established, relationships can withstand challenges and grow stronger over time.

Effective communication is another critical component. Listening actively, expressing empathy, and being open to feedback are essential skills for nurturing relationships. Clear, respectful communication helps resolve conflicts and misunderstandings, strengthening the bond between individuals.

Equally important is the ability to navigate life's challenges together. Facing difficulties as a team builds resilience and deepens the connection. Whether it's supporting a partner through a career change, helping a friend through a tough time, or working through family issues, the ability to lean on each other fosters a sense of solidarity and mutual strength.

In conclusion, resilient relationships are built on trust, effective communication, and mutual support. By investing time and effort into these aspects, we create a network of strong, supportive connections that enhance our prosperity and well-being.

5

Chapter 5: Economic Growth and Personal Prosperity

Economic growth plays a significant role in personal prosperity. A stable economy provides opportunities for employment, entrepreneurship, and financial stability, enabling individuals to pursue their goals and aspirations. However, personal prosperity is not solely defined by economic wealth; it encompasses a broader spectrum of well-being.

Achieving financial stability is a crucial aspect of personal prosperity. It allows individuals to meet their basic needs, invest in their future, and enjoy a sense of security. Financial literacy, budgeting, and saving are essential skills for managing personal finances and achieving economic well-being.

Moreover, economic growth can facilitate access to education, healthcare, and other resources that contribute to overall well-being. When societies invest in these areas, they create an environment where individuals can thrive and pursue their aspirations. Economic policies that promote equity and inclusion ensure that the benefits of growth are shared, fostering a more prosperous society.

While economic growth is important, it is not the sole determinant of personal prosperity. True prosperity encompasses physical health, mental well-being, strong relationships, and a sense of purpose. By balancing economic pursuits with other aspects of well-being, individuals can achieve a holistic sense of prosperity.

6

Chapter 6: Health as a Cornerstone of Prosperity

Health is a fundamental pillar of prosperity, influencing our ability to pursue our goals, enjoy life, and contribute to society. A healthy body and mind provide the foundation for a fulfilling and prosperous life.

Physical health is essential for maintaining energy, strength, and resilience. Regular exercise, balanced nutrition, and preventive healthcare are key components of physical well-being. By prioritizing our physical health, we ensure that we have the vitality to engage fully with life's opportunities and challenges.

Mental health is equally important. Emotional well-being, stress management, and mental resilience are crucial for navigating life's ups and downs. Practices such as mindfulness, meditation, and therapy can help maintain mental health, fostering a sense of balance and fulfillment.

Moreover, health is interconnected with other aspects of prosperity. Strong relationships, a sense of purpose, and economic stability all contribute to overall well-being. When we prioritize our health, we create a foundation for achieving our goals and enjoying a prosperous life.

In conclusion, health is a cornerstone of prosperity. By nurturing our physical and mental well-being, we create a solid foundation for a fulfilling and prosperous life.

7

Chapter 7: The Power of Purpose

Having a sense of purpose is a powerful driver of prosperity. It gives meaning to our actions, motivates us to pursue our goals, and provides a sense of fulfillment. A clear sense of purpose helps us navigate life's challenges and stay focused on what truly matters.

Purpose can be found in various aspects of life, such as career, relationships, personal growth, and contributions to society. It is the guiding force that shapes our decisions and actions, aligning them with our values and aspirations. When we have a sense of purpose, we are more likely to experience a deep sense of satisfaction and fulfillment.

Moreover, purpose fosters resilience. It provides a sense of direction and motivation, helping us persevere through difficult times. When we are driven by a clear purpose, we are more likely to overcome obstacles and achieve our goals.

In addition to personal fulfillment, purpose has a broader impact on society. Individuals who are motivated by a sense of purpose are more likely to contribute positively to their communities, driving social and economic progress. By aligning our personal goals with a greater purpose, we create a ripple effect that enhances collective prosperity.

8

Chapter 8: The Role of Community

Community plays a vital role in our sense of prosperity and well-being. Being part of a supportive and inclusive community provides a sense of belonging, fosters social connections, and creates opportunities for collaboration and growth.

A strong community offers mutual support and encouragement. It provides a network of individuals who share common interests, values, and goals. This sense of connection enhances our well-being, offering comfort during challenging times and amplifying our joys.

Moreover, communities drive collective progress. When individuals come together to address common challenges and pursue shared goals, they create positive change. Community initiatives can promote education, health, economic development, and social cohesion, fostering a more prosperous society.

Additionally, being part of a community fosters a sense of responsibility and accountability. When we contribute to the well-being of our community, we create a positive impact that benefits everyone. This sense of collective responsibility enhances our sense of purpose and fulfillment.

In conclusion, community plays a crucial role in our sense of prosperity and well-being. By being active members of our communities, we build supportive networks, drive collective progress, and foster a sense of belonging and purpose. A strong community enriches our lives, making us feel connected

CHAPTER 8: THE ROLE OF COMMUNITY

and valued.

9

Chapter 9: The Balance of Work and Life

Striking a balance between work and life is essential for achieving true prosperity. While work provides financial stability and a sense of purpose, it is equally important to prioritize personal well-being, relationships, and leisure activities. Achieving this balance requires mindful planning and self-awareness.

Setting boundaries between work and personal life is a key strategy. Establishing clear work hours and creating a designated workspace can help maintain this separation. It is important to disconnect from work during personal time, allowing for relaxation and rejuvenation. This boundary-setting fosters a healthy work-life balance, reducing stress and enhancing overall well-being.

Moreover, prioritizing self-care is essential. Engaging in activities that bring joy and relaxation, such as hobbies, exercise, and spending time with loved ones, contributes to a sense of fulfillment and happiness. Self-care practices help recharge our energy, making us more productive and focused during work hours.

In addition, fostering a supportive work environment can enhance work-life balance. Employers can promote flexible work arrangements, encourage regular breaks, and support employees' well-being. A positive work culture that values work-life balance enhances job satisfaction and overall prosperity.

In conclusion, balancing work and life is crucial for achieving holistic

CHAPTER 9: THE BALANCE OF WORK AND LIFE

prosperity. By setting boundaries, prioritizing self-care, and fostering a supportive work environment, individuals can enjoy a fulfilling and prosperous life.

10

Chapter 10: The Influence of Technology on Prosperity

Technology has a profound impact on our lives and prosperity. It offers unprecedented opportunities for innovation, communication, and access to information. However, it also presents challenges that require mindful navigation.

One of the most significant benefits of technology is its ability to connect people across the globe. Social media, video conferencing, and messaging apps allow us to maintain relationships and collaborate with others regardless of distance. This connectivity fosters a sense of community and collaboration, enhancing our prosperity.

Moreover, technology drives innovation and economic growth. It enables the development of new industries, products, and services, creating job opportunities and improving quality of life. Embracing technological advancements can lead to personal and professional growth, fostering a prosperous future.

However, it is important to navigate the challenges posed by technology. Issues such as digital addiction, privacy concerns, and the impact of automation on employment require careful consideration. Mindful use of technology, setting boundaries, and staying informed about its impact can help mitigate these challenges.

CHAPTER 10: THE INFLUENCE OF TECHNOLOGY ON PROSPERITY

In conclusion, technology has a significant influence on our prosperity. By leveraging its benefits and navigating its challenges mindfully, we can harness its potential to enhance our lives and achieve true prosperity.

11

Chapter 11: The Impact of Environment on Well-being

Our environment profoundly influences our sense of well-being and prosperity. The spaces we inhabit, the air we breathe, and the natural surroundings all contribute to our physical and mental health. Creating a healthy and supportive environment is essential for achieving holistic prosperity.

Indoor environments, such as homes and workplaces, play a crucial role in our well-being. Clean, well-ventilated spaces with natural light and ergonomic design enhance comfort and productivity. Personalizing our spaces with elements that bring joy and relaxation, such as plants, art, and comfortable furniture, can boost our mood and reduce stress.

Outdoor environments also have a significant impact on our well-being. Spending time in nature, whether through walks in the park, hiking, or gardening, has been shown to reduce stress, improve mood, and enhance overall health. Access to green spaces and clean air is essential for our physical and mental well-being.

Moreover, environmental sustainability is crucial for long-term prosperity. Protecting natural resources, reducing waste, and promoting sustainable practices ensure a healthy planet for future generations. By adopting eco-friendly habits, such as recycling, conserving energy, and supporting

CHAPTER 11: THE IMPACT OF ENVIRONMENT ON WELL-BEING

sustainable products, we contribute to a prosperous and sustainable future.

In conclusion, our environment plays a vital role in our well-being and prosperity. Creating healthy and supportive indoor and outdoor spaces, and promoting environmental sustainability, enhances our quality of life and fosters holistic prosperity.

12

Chapter 12: Cultivating Mindfulness and Presence

Mindfulness and presence are powerful practices that enhance our well-being and prosperity. They involve being fully present in the moment, cultivating awareness, and embracing life with a sense of gratitude and acceptance.

Mindfulness practices, such as meditation, deep breathing, and mindful movement, help calm the mind and reduce stress. By focusing on the present moment, we can let go of worries about the past or future, fostering a sense of peace and clarity. Regular mindfulness practice enhances mental resilience, emotional stability, and overall well-being.

Moreover, mindfulness encourages us to savor the simple joys of life. Whether it's enjoying a meal, spending time with loved ones, or appreciating nature, being fully present allows us to experience life more deeply and meaningfully. This mindful presence fosters a sense of gratitude and fulfillment, enhancing our prosperity.

In addition, mindfulness improves our relationships. By being fully present and attentive in our interactions, we strengthen our connections and enhance communication. Mindful listening, empathy, and non-judgmental awareness create a deeper sense of understanding and trust in our relationships.

In conclusion, cultivating mindfulness and presence is essential for achieving holistic prosperity. By embracing the present moment and practicing mindfulness, we enhance our mental and emotional well-being, strengthen our relationships, and enjoy a more fulfilling and prosperous life.

13

Chapter 13: The Journey of Personal Growth

Personal growth is a lifelong journey that contributes to our sense of prosperity and fulfillment. It involves continuous learning, self-discovery, and the pursuit of our passions and aspirations. Embracing personal growth enriches our lives, making us more resilient, adaptable, and fulfilled.

Self-awareness is the foundation of personal growth. Understanding our strengths, weaknesses, values, and motivations allows us to make informed decisions and pursue goals that align with our true selves. Reflective practices, such as journaling, meditation, and seeking feedback, help cultivate self-awareness and guide our growth journey.

Moreover, setting and pursuing meaningful goals is essential for personal growth. Goals provide direction and purpose, motivating us to take action and overcome challenges. Whether it's developing new skills, advancing in our careers, or pursuing personal passions, setting clear, achievable goals fosters a sense of accomplishment and fulfillment.

In addition, embracing change and challenges is crucial for growth. Life is filled with uncertainties and obstacles, but these experiences offer valuable lessons and opportunities for development. By adopting a growth mindset and viewing challenges as opportunities for learning, we build resilience and

CHAPTER 13: THE JOURNEY OF PERSONAL GROWTH

adaptability, enhancing our prosperity.

In conclusion, personal growth is a continuous journey that enriches our lives and contributes to our prosperity. By cultivating self-awareness, setting meaningful goals, and embracing change, we achieve a sense of fulfillment and enjoy a prosperous life.

14

Chapter 14: The Importance of Gratitude

Gratitude is a powerful practice that enhances our well-being and prosperity. It involves recognizing and appreciating the positive aspects of our lives, fostering a sense of contentment and joy. Cultivating gratitude enriches our lives, making us more resilient, optimistic, and fulfilled.

Regularly practicing gratitude helps shift our focus from what we lack to what we have. This positive perspective fosters a sense of abundance and contentment, reducing stress and enhancing our overall well-being. Simple practices, such as keeping a gratitude journal, expressing thanks to others, and reflecting on positive experiences, can help cultivate a habit of gratitude.

Moreover, gratitude improves our relationships. Expressing appreciation to others strengthens our connections and fosters a sense of trust and mutual support. Gratitude enhances empathy and understanding, creating a positive and supportive social environment.

In addition, gratitude fosters resilience. By focusing on the positive aspects of our lives, we develop a more optimistic outlook and are better equipped to navigate challenges. Gratitude helps us find meaning and purpose, even in difficult times, enhancing our mental and emotional well-being.

In conclusion, gratitude is a powerful practice that enhances our well-being and prosperity. By regularly practicing gratitude, we cultivate a sense of contentment, strengthen our relationships, and build resilience, fostering a

CHAPTER 14: THE IMPORTANCE OF GRATITUDE

fulfilling and prosperous life.

15

Chapter 15: The Synergy of Growth, Health, and Relationships

The true essence of prosperity lies in the synergy of growth, health, and relationships. These interconnected aspects of our lives work together to create a holistic sense of well-being and fulfillment. By nurturing each of these areas, we achieve a balanced and prosperous life.

Personal growth provides the foundation for a fulfilling life. Continuous learning, self-discovery, and the pursuit of our passions enrich our lives and enhance our resilience. When we invest in our growth, we become more adaptable, motivated, and purposeful.

Health is the cornerstone of our well-being. Physical and mental health enable us to pursue our goals, enjoy life, and navigate challenges. By prioritizing our health through proper nutrition, exercise, and self-care, we create a strong foundation for a prosperous life.

Strong relationships are essential for our sense of belonging and support. Trust, effective communication, and mutual support create resilient connections that enrich our lives. By investing in our relationships, we build a network of support and encouragement that enhances our prosperity.

In conclusion, the synergy of growth, health, and relationships is the key to achieving true prosperity. By nurturing each of these aspects, we create a balanced and fulfilling life, enjoying a sense of well-being, purpose, and

CHAPTER 15: THE SYNERGY OF GROWTH, HEALTH, AND RELATIONSHIPS

connection.

Confluence of Prosperity: Weaving Threads of Growth, Health, and Relationship Strengthening

In "Confluence of Prosperity," we explore the intricate tapestry of true prosperity, delving into the essential threads that weave together growth, health, and relationship strengthening. This book offers a comprehensive guide to achieving a balanced and fulfilling life, emphasizing the interconnectedness of personal growth, physical and mental well-being, and resilient relationships.

Through 15 engaging chapters, we journey through the foundations of prosperity, the role of education, the interconnection of physical and mental health, and the importance of resilient relationships. Each chapter provides valuable insights and practical strategies for nurturing these aspects of our lives, creating a harmonious and prosperous existence.

From the balance of work and life to the influence of technology, the impact of the environment, and the power of mindfulness, this book addresses the various dimensions of prosperity. It highlights the significance of gratitude, personal growth, and community, offering a holistic approach to achieving a prosperous and fulfilling life.

"Confluence of Prosperity" is a compelling read for anyone seeking to enrich their life, strengthen their relationships, and achieve a deeper sense of well-being. With a blend of insightful reflections and actionable advice, this book serves as a guide to weaving the threads of growth, health, and relationship strengthening into a vibrant tapestry of prosperity.

www.ingramcontent.com/pod-product-compliance
Lightning Source LLC
LaVergne TN
LVHW020740090526
838202LV00057BA/6140